At the Museum

Practicing the YOO Sound

Dylan Karsten

Rosen PHONICS READERS

Rosen Classroom™

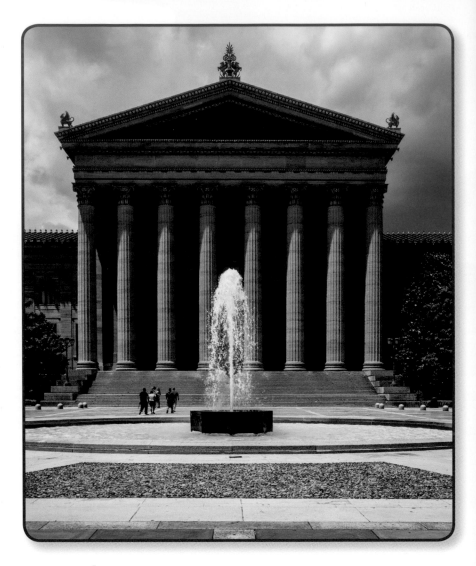

My class is going
to an art museum.
The museum is huge!

We wear our usual uniforms.
Our uniforms are cute.

There is music in the museum.
I love music!

I see unusual art.
This is an unusual shape.

I see beautiful art, too.
What a beautiful painting!

I see art shaped like a cube.
That cube is huge!

I see a statue.

That statue is huge, too.

This statue is a human.
I am a human!

This statue is a unicorn.
Do you like unicorns?

Is this art from the future?

I loved the museum!
Do you like art museums?